Flowers

June Loves

CHELSEA CLUBHOUSE

An Imprint of Chelsea House Publishers
A Haights Cross Communications Company
Philadelphia

First published in 2005 by
MACMILLAN EDUCATION AUSTRALIA PTY LTD
627 Chapel Street, South Yarra 3141

Associated companies and representatives throughout the world.

National Library of Australia
Cataloguing-in-Publication data

Library of Congress Cataloging-in-Publication Data
       Loves, June.
       Flowers / June Loves.
       p. cm. – (Plants)
       Includes index.
       ISBN 0-7910-8265-2
       1. Flowers – Juvenile literature. 2. Plants – Juvenile literature. I. Title.
       QK49.L84 2004

                                        582.13–dc22

Edited by Anna Fern
Text and cover design by Christine Deering
Page layout by Christine Deering
Photo research by Legend Images
Illustrations by Melissa Webb

Printed in China
Acknowledgements
The author and the publisher are grateful to the following for permission to reproduce
copyright material:

Cover photograph: Colourful flowers, courtesy of Photodisc.

Mike Langford/AUSCAPE, p. 7; Reg Morrison/AUSCAPE, p. 29; Australian Picture
Library, pp. 18, 19, 28, 30; Australian Picture Library/Corbis, p. 14 (bottom); Corbis
Digital Stock, p. 20; The DW Stock Picture Library, pp. 8, 14 (top), 17; Getty Images, p.
15 (top); Getty Images/Stone, p. 13; Photodisc, pp. 1, 3, 4, 5, 9, 10, 11, 15 (bottom), 21,
22, 27; PhotoEssentials, p. 6; Photolibrary.com, pp. 12, 16, 23; Sarah Saunders, p. 26.

While every care has been taken to trace and acknowledge copyright, the publisher
tenders their apologies for any accidental infringement where copyright has proved
untraceable. Where the attempt has been unsuccessful, the publisher welcomes
information that would redress the situation.

Contents

Plants

Plants are living things. They grow all over the world, in hot and cold places.

Some plants grow in water.

Flowers

Flowers are parts of plants that can be colorful and eye-catching. A flower is the part of the plant that makes seeds.

People enjoy growing colorful flowering plants in their gardens.

Where Flowering Plants Grow

Flowering plants grow in most parts of the world. They can grow in **rain forests**, **deserts**, and cold mountains.

These orchids grow in damp, warm rain forests.

Some flowering plants grow better at certain times of the year. **Alpine plants** grow where there are long cold winters, and short summers. In the short summers, the plants make their flowers and seeds quickly.

Alpine plants grow close to the ground for protection from strong, cold winds.

Kinds of Flowers

There are many different kinds, sizes, shapes, and colors of flowers. Some flowers have petals that are all shaped the same. Other flowers have petals with different shapes.

These snapdragons have petals with different shapes.

Wildflowers

Wildflowers are the flowers that have always grown in a particular place. Many wildflowers are grown by gardeners in other parts of the world, far from where the flowers came from.

These wildflowers are growing in the mountain countryside.

Garden Flowers

Some flowers are specially grown by gardeners for their beautiful colors and perfume.

This rose was specially grown by gardeners.

Many Flowers in One

Some flowers look like one flower, but they are really made up of many flowers. Daisies and sunflowers have large centers. The centers are made up of many tiny flowers.

Inside the ring of petals of this daisy flower, there are many small flowers.

Parts of a Flowering Plant

The leaves of a flowering plant collect energy from the sun to make food inside the plant. The **roots** hold the plant in the soil, and collect water and **minerals** from the soil.

flower

stem

bud

leaves

roots

Poppy plants produce beautiful papery flowers.

12

The parts of a plant that make seeds for new plants are called **stamens** and **pistils**. They are found in the center of the flower.

petal

stamen

pollen

pistil

The petals of poppy flowers can be many different colors.

How Flowering Plants Grow

All flowering plants grow from seeds. A seed contains a tiny plant and the food it needs to grow.

A seed is planted in the soil. The seed sprouts a root and a **shoot**.

The flowers grow into **fruits** which contain seeds for more plants.

When the leaves on the shoot open, they collect energy from the sun so that the plant can make its own food.

The plant grows and flowers.

New Plants from Shoots and Bulbs

Some flowering plants grow new plants by sending out shoots. The shoots grow roots of their own and become new plants.

These shoots with new plants have grown from a strawberry plant.

Other flowering plants grow from **bulbs** under
the ground. The bulbs can divide up to make
new plants.

**These jonquil bulbs have divided
up to make more jonquil plants.**

How Flowers Make Seeds

Flowers contain male and female parts. The male parts, called stamens, make a special dust called pollen. The female parts, called the pistils, contain tiny eggs. To make seeds, the eggs in the flower need to join with some pollen.

petal

stamen

pollen

pistil

Flowers have female parts, called pistils, and male parts, called stamens.

Pollen is carried from one flower to another by insects, birds, or the wind. The pollen falls onto the sticky pistil and joins up with an egg. This is called **pollination**. The flower grows into a fruit. Inside the fruit, the egg grows into a seed.

fruit containing seeds

flower petals have fallen away

When the fruit is ripe, the seeds inside are ready to grow into new plants.

Helpful Animals and Insects

Many animals and insects are attracted by the beautiful colors and scent of flowers. They feed on the sweet **nectar** inside flowers.

Hummingbirds feed on flower nectar.

When an insect or animal visits a flower to feed, dusty pollen can fall onto its body. At the next flower, some pollen may fall off onto the pistil of the flower. In this way, insect and animal visitors help with pollination.

This bee has pollen stuck to its hairy body.

Growing Flowers

Growing your own flowers can be fun. You need to dig, plant, weed, and water to take care of your flower garden. Like most other plants, flowering plants need soil, water, and light to grow well.

You need to water your plants every day.

You can grow flowers from seeds, or you can buy young plants, called seedlings, from shops. Plant them in pots, or in the garden. Add plant food to the soil to help your plants grow well.

Before you plant your flowers in the garden, you should turn the soil over.

Grow Some Spring Bulbs

Flowers such as tulips and daffodils grow from bulbs. Food stored in the bulb feeds the bud inside it.

What you need:

- one tulip or daffodil bulb
- craft knife
- empty yogurt container
- empty jar
- water

What to do:

1 Ask an adult to help you cut the bottom out of a yogurt container with the craft knife. The bulb should be able to sit in the yogurt container without falling out.

2 Fit the yogurt container into the top of the jar.

3 Place the bulb, pointed end up, into the yogurt container. Fill the jar with water to cover the bottom of the bulb.

4 Keep the jar in a dark place until the roots are 4 inches (10 centimeters) long. Remove it to a light place and watch your bulb bloom.

Tips for Gardeners

Flowers can be grown indoors and outdoors, in pots or planted in the garden.

- Flowers in pots and window boxes can dry out quickly. Water them every day in warm weather.

- Pull out any weeds so that they do not take over your flowers.

You can grow a beautiful garden almost anywhere.

- A layer of **mulch** helps keep the soil moist and stops weeds from growing.

- Always wash your hands and scrub your nails when you have finished handling soil.

This garden is filled with colorful spring flowers.

Useful Flowers

For thousands of years, people have used flowers to flavor their food. Rose petals are used to flavor some sweets. Spicy cloves used in curries and other foods are the buds of flowers.

The orange stamens of these crocus flowers are sold as the flavoring saffron.

Flowers, such as lavender, are used to make skin-care products and perfume. Some parts of flowers are used to make medicine.

This is a crop of lavender flowers at a lavender farm.

Amazing Flowers

The biggest flower in the world is the rafflesia, which grows in the rain forests of Southeast Asia. It measures about 3 feet (1 meter) across. It is pollinated by flies, which are attracted by its smell of rotten meat.

The rafflesia is a rain forest plant.

Glossary

alpine plant a plant that grows in high mountain areas

bud top of a shoot or branch where new leaves or flowers grow

bulb an underground stem that stores food and water for a plant

desert a very dry place with few plants

fruit part of a flowering plant that contains seeds

minerals chemicals in the soil that plants need to grow

mulch a layer of chopped-up leaves or other plant materials to help stop the soil from drying out and stop weeds from growing

nectar sweet liquid made by flowers which attracts animals and insects

pistil the female part of a flower which contains eggs

pollen fine yellow dust made in the center of a flower

pollination movement of pollen from one flower to another

rain forest a thick forest with heavy rainfall, and which is full of living things

root part of a plant that grows down into the soil and takes in water and nutrients

shoot young branch or stem of a plant

stamen the part of the flower that makes pollen

Index